Original title:
Wheaten Pods Inside the Mermaid Deck

Copyright © 2025 Swan Charm

Author: Sara Säde
ISBN HARDBACK: 978-1-80563-057-9
ISBN PAPERBACK: 978-1-80564-578-8

Nectar of the Mermaid's Gardens

In gardens where the shadows play,
Mermaids weave their dreams in spray.
With petals bright, their laughter swirls,
Enchanting songs of ocean pearls.

Beneath the waves, sweet nectar flows,
In every tide, the magic grows.
A shimmer bright, like stars at sea,
Whispers of joy, wild and free.

Emerald leaves and sapphire light,
Dance in the depths, a wondrous sight.
Where coral blooms in soft embrace,
A secret world, a hidden place.

In twilight's hush, the waters gleam,
Crafting the fabric of a dream.
With every breath of ocean air,
The mermaids sing with tender care.

Trinity of Earth, Water, and Whimsy

In whispers soft, the earth does sigh,
Underneath a vast, blue sky.
Water flows in silver streams,
Binding all with gentle dreams.

A trinity of elements grand,
Harmony in every land.
The laughter of the trees above,
Encircles all with boundless love.

Through every drop and every stone,
The stories of the world are grown.
From mountain high to ocean low,
Life's vibrant dance begins to flow.

In whimsy's touch, the magic's near,
Nature's voice is sweet and clear.
The dance of shadows, light, and mirth,
A sacred bond with all of earth.

Currents of Corn and Coral

In fields where golden corn does sway,
The ocean calls, pulls hearts away.
Coral reefs in colors bright,
Beneath the waves, a wondrous sight.

Currents meet where soil and sea,
Merge in a dance of harmony.
From earthen roots to salty spray,
Life's symphony calls night and day.

With every grain, a story spun,
Of sunlit days and waters run.
The pulse of life, both raw and true,
In every drop and every dew.

As tides roll in with gentle grace,
We find the echoes of our place.
In corn and coral, heartstrings twine,
A legacy of earth divine.

Siren's Harvest in the Ocean Deep

In depths where sunlight softly fades,
The siren's song in twilight wades.
With treasures spun from ocean's heart,
She gathers secrets, sets apart.

Each shell a story, woven tight,
Of sunlit days and starry night.
In whispered tones, the secrets keep,
The harvest of the ocean deep.

In shimmering waves, her dreams take flight,
Adorned with jewels, ever bright.
From currents wide to shores so steep,
The siren's call, an ancient sweep.

With every tide, a tale unfolds,
Of ancient magic and legends old.
Her laughter twirls in ocean's sweep,
The siren's harvest, ours to reap.

Castaways of the Sea's Abundance

Upon the shore where shadows blend,
Waves whisper tales of journeys wend,
Crews of sailors, lost in dreams,
Carried by time's relentless streams.

Seagulls circle, cries of despair,
Echoes linger in salty air,
Driftwood speaks of distant lands,
Where hope rose high on golden sands.

Castaways with hearts of stone,
In the ocean's arms, they moan,
Yet treasures lie beneath the tide,
In secrets deep where legends bide.

With each sunrise, a chance to soar,
To find the hearth on a distant shore,
For every tear the ocean spent,
A ship shall rise, a soul revent.

In twilight's glow, they chart their fate,
While starlit waves illuminate,
A promise beckons, fierce and wide,
As castaways reclaim their pride.

Sown Treasures Where Water Dances

In secret glades where rivers twirl,
Sun-kissed seeds begin to unfurl,
Lilies sway in gentle grace,
Mirrored pools their shimmering face.

Fishes flash in colors bright,
A ballet held in dappled light,
Ripples whispering sweet refrains,
Of hidden wealth in nature's veins.

Every drop, a story spun,
Of battles lost, of glories won,
Where mermaids weave their songs of old,
In waters where the brave are bold.

As twilight dips its colors low,
Magic stirs in currents flow,
Where hearts entwine like vines at rest,
In nature's chest, the seeds are blessed.

The treasures sown in liquid dreams,
Beckon softly, or so it seems,
To those who dare to delve and dive,
And find the truth where waters strive.

The Melodies of Grain and Ocean

In fields of gold where breezes sigh,
The ocean's whispers reach the sky,
A symphony of earth and tide,
Where dreams of harvest dreams abide.

Waves crash softly on the shore,
Notes of laughter rise and soar,
Grains sway gently in sunlit dance,
Each seed a fate, each gust a chance.

Harmony in wind's embrace,
A melody time won't erase,
As salt and soil find their way,
In nature's tune, they both shall play.

The fishermen hum their lore so grand,
While farmers toil on sun-kissed land,
In unity, the rhythms meet,
A world replete, a song so sweet.

Together bound by earth and sea,
In simple grace, we wander free,
For in each heart, a story weaves,
Of melodies that life receives.

Enchantment Under Aquatic Stars

In moonlit depths, the shadows glide,
Where silent secrets softly hide,
Beneath the waves, a world unfolds,
In dances told by creatures bold.

Stars above in velvet skies,
Reflect like dreams in fishy eyes,
Their glimmers pierce the ocean vast,
As time drips by like dreams long past.

Tales of magic swirl in blue,
Where echoes of the ancients grew,
Anemones sway, and currents play,
As myths are born in ocean's sway.

Underwater realms of molten light,
Where day dissolves into the night,
Enchantments hum in rhythmic flow,
With whispers shared that few will know.

And in this realm, we lose our care,
With every breath, a gentle prayer,
For in the dark, a spark ignites,
Enchantment thrives in starry nights.

Merfolk's Picnic on Sandy Shores

Beneath the waves, where secrets dwell,
Merfolk gather, tales to tell.
With shells and seaweed, spread so bright,
They feast on laughter, day and night.

Crabs dance lightly, in the sand,
With starfish clapping, it's quite grand.
The ocean's tune, a soft refrain,
Echoes sweetly, like warm rain.

Bright jellyfish glide, a shimmering show,
While dolphins leap, putting on a blow.
With salted breeze, and sunlit gleams,
They twirl in joy, lost in their dreams.

The tide brings gifts from far-off lands,
A treasure trove of nature's hands.
With every bite, and every cheer,
They celebrate the ocean near.

As stars appear in evening's glow,
The merfolk hum, their voices low.
Under the moon, their hearts take wing,
In perfect harmony, they sing.

Undersea Gold in Silken Bellies

In the depths where the sun's light fades,
Mermaids hide golden treasures, unafraid.
With shimmering scales like sunsets bound,
They guard the secrets beneath the ground.

With flicks of tails, they weave and sway,
In gardens of coral, where colors play.
Silken bellies, adorned with pearls,
Twirl through the currents, like whirlpools.

The laughter of fish, a glittering choir,
Echoes softly, like a gentle fire.
Each treasure glimmers, in glinting waves,
Guarded by magic that the ocean saves.

Through caverns dark, and shadows deep,
The merfolk dance, secrets they keep.
With every flippered, rhythmic beat,
Their stories of riches are bittersweet.

At hidden dawns, when light does creep,
They gather the gold, in silence sweep.
With dreams of worlds above the waves,
They cherish the beauty that the sea saves.

Abundant Shores of Silken Dreams

Upon the shore, where sea foam plays,
The merfolk wander in drifting haze.
With eyes of wonder, and hearts so free,
They weave their dreams, like sea and plea.

Golden sands beneath their feet,
Whisper tales of love, soft and sweet.
Glistening shells, and tides that roam,
Are gifts from the sea, their cherished home.

They gather at dusk, when the stars appear,
Sharing wishes, with nothing to fear.
Of ships and skies, and lands afar,
Their laughter echoes, like drifting stars.

The rhythm of waves, a calming song,
Binds their spirits, where they belong.
In every tide, in every stream,
They find adventure, and silken dreams.

So when the moon reflects on night,
The merfolk dance, in pure delight.
Embracing love, and joy unclaimed,
In abundant shores, their hearts remain.

The Grains of Tide and Time

In every grain of sand, a story lies,
Written by waves and whispered sighs.
Tide and time, in a constant dance,
Shape the shore with each fleeting glance.

Merfolk gather, with tales to share,
Of lost ships and treasures rare.
With every ebb, and every flow,
They celebrate life, in sun's warm glow.

Time flows softly, like currents wide,
Leaving memories where secrets bide.
The moon's soft pull, a celestial rhyme,
Guides the dance of the grains of time.

Whispers of ancient, fill the air,
With each tide's kiss, love's touch is rare.
As the stars blink down in the deep,
The merfolk dream, while the world sleeps.

Through ages past, and futures bright,
They honor the past, in starlit night.
For every grain of tide and time,
Holds a heartbeat, a story sublime.

The Grainy Soliloquy of the Ocean

Waves whisper tales of yore,
Sands like secrets on the shore.
Each grain a story, small and round,
Echoes of silence, softly found.

The horizon beckons, vast and wide,
Where dreams and reality collide.
In twilight's glow, the sea does sigh,
Underneath the painted sky.

A ship's sail flutters, a fleeting ghost,
While seabirds circle, a tranquil host.
With every tide, the past returns,
In the ocean's heart, a fire burns.

Footprints left, then washed away,
By the gentle hand of a new day.
The grains of time, both rough and smooth,
In the ocean's dance, we find our groove.

As the sun dips low, the colors gleam,
In this grainy world, we dare to dream.
The ocean speaks, a timeless song,
In the rippling current, we belong.

Beneath the Surface of the Shimmering Sea

Beneath the waves, where shadows glide,
A world awakes, the tide's soft ride.
Coral castles, vibrant and bright,
Hide secrets deeper than the night.

Fish dart swift like fleeting thoughts,
In colors that time has surely wrought.
Anemones dance, their arms unfurl,
As the ocean spins its timeless whirl.

A whisper of currents, a lover's breath,
Carries the tales of life and death.
Beneath this gleam, a kingdom thrives,
In every bubble, a soul survives.

The echoes of laughter in watery halls,
Resound through the tides, as twilight falls.
Mirrors of starlight, shimmering and bright,
Below the surface, spells of night.

In the tranquil depths where dreams convene,
Nature's wonders weave silver and green.
Beneath the waves that ebb and flow,
Lies a world where magic continuously grows.

A Sea of Harvests in Glistening Hues

Harvests rich in emerald and blue,
A tapestry woven, both old and new.
Kelp dances softly, swaying in grace,
Under the sun's warm, loving embrace.

Netting glimmers in fishermen's hands,
As tides reveal their bountiful strands.
Shells like jewels, smooth and rare,
Whisper of journeys, of love and care.

The seabed's treasure, a feast for the wise,
Mirth from the ocean's vibrant guise.
Crisp sea air carries laughter and cheer,
In this harvest sea, love draws near.

With each gentle swell, a story unfolds,
Of courage and dreams, that time beholds.
In comb and shell, a voyage begun,
Together we laugh, beneath the bright sun.

As boat sails drift on a shimmering tide,
With every catch, the joy cannot hide.
For in a sea where glistening hues play,
Every moment is magic, come what may.

Tidal Echoes of Earth and Water

The pulse of the sea, a heartbeat strong,
In tidal echoes, we all belong.
Sand meets sea, in soft embrace,
Whispering secrets of time and space.

Glistening waters, a mirror to sky,
Reflecting tales that never die.
Each wave a voice that calls aloud,
With thunderous joy, both fierce and proud.

From distant shores, the stories sail,
Carried by winds in a bittersweet wail.
With every crash, the earth takes flight,
In the union of day and night.

The ocean's breath, a haunting tune,
Plays in whispers beneath the moon.
Nature's symphony, harmonious grand,
Binding the earth with a gentle hand.

Across the shores, life ebbs and flows,
Each step a journey, as the water goes.
In tidal rhythms, we find our way,
In echoes of earth, where we choose to stay.

The Edge of Shoreline Delights

Waves dance upon the golden sand,
Whispers of secrets from distant lands.
A gull's cry punctuates the air,
While seafoam spirals without care.

Children chase the frothy tide,
Laughter mingling, hearts open wide.
Shells gleam like jewels in the sun,
In moments caught, life's magic spun.

The horizon stretches, limitless and vast,
Footprints fading, memories cast.
Breezes carry tales from afar,
Underneath the twinkling stars.

Seagrapes sway with the evening breeze,
Nature's symphony sings with ease.
The salty air lifts dreams to soar,
On the edge where sea meets shore.

Here where water and dreams entwine,
All worries fade, and hearts align.
In this haven, we find our light,
At the edge of day and night.

Flavors of Salt in Harvested Dreams

Salt on lips, a memory sweet,
From harvest nights where spirits meet.
Windswept fields, the stars aglow,
Whispers of tales that ebb and flow.

Baskets brimmed with treasures fair,
Golden grains, the heart laid bare.
A toast to the sea and land we share,
In laughter's echo, joy lays bare.

From sun-kissed shores to fields so wide,
Every flavor with love applied.
Gathered dreams in a moonlit bowl,
Tales of adventures, woven whole.

With every sip, the past awakes,
As tasted memories take their stakes.
A sip of salt, a dash of grace,
In every corner, a warm embrace.

Harvested dreams in salty air,
Remind us all, we bloom with care.
Together we stand, in this shared delight,
As flavors dance in soft moonlight.

The Marine Midas and His Fields of Gold

Beneath the waves, a treasure sleeps,
In golden fields where magic sweeps.
The Marine Midas, bold and true,
Turns grain to gold where waters blue.

His touch transforms the humble tide,
Every ship a fortune rides.
In currents deep, the secrets flow,
Riches born where restless waters glow.

Seashell crowns and coral rings,
Woven from the joy that singing brings.
Harvest of dreams from ocean floors,
Abundant wealth that forever pours.

Reflections shimmer in the sun,
A realm of fortune, never done.
With every wave, his legacy grows,
In tides of wonder that the ocean knows.

Gold beneath, and silver above,
A feast prepared with ocean's love.
The Marine Midas, with hands of fate,
In his kingdom of waves, we celebrate.

Wandering Spirits of Grainy Harmony

In fields where whispers gently roam,
Spirits dance, the earth their home.
Grainy harmony in twilight's hymn,
Soft melodies where shadows dim.

Chasing echoes in the twilight glow,
They weave through stalks where wild winds blow.
Each rustling leaf, a tale unfolds,
Of ages past and secrets told.

Beneath the moon, the shadows play,
As night ignites the faded day.
With hearts entwined in nature's song,
Wandering spirits where we belong.

Together they sway, the stars their guide,
In the dance of worlds, they take their stride.
Echoes of laughter, lost and found,
In this harmony, magic abounds.

They bless the grain with gentle hands,
Nurturing dreams where life expands.
In woven fields, we find our peace,
With wandering spirits, our joys increase.

Fertile Dreams of Aquatic Realms

Beneath the waves where secrets lie,
The dances of the fish nearby,
Dreams weave through currents, soft and bright,
In the depths, the world ignites.

Coral castles in colors bold,
Guard treasures that the ocean holds,
With whispers of the tides that sweep,
These visions stir from shadows deep.

Glimmers of hope in the ocean's embrace,
Dance like sunbeams in a silken trace,
Each ripple sings to those who dare,
To dream of worlds that linger there.

Creatures waltz in a watery ball,
Their movements etched, a symphonic call,
In harmony with the moon's soft gaze,
Life flourishes in the ocean's maze.

So dive into dreams spun from the sea,
Where every wave holds a memory,
In these fertile realms, let spirits soar,
And find the magic forevermore.

Whispers of the Submerged Harvest

In twilight's glow, the sea's embrace,
Whispers mingle in calmest space,
Voices rise from the depths unseen,
Harvests awaited in waters green.

Across the field of tides that sway,
Life's bounty rustles, day by day,
Every echo, a tale retold,
In the folds of waves, treasures unfold.

Starfish glisten on sandy shores,
As currents gather what nature pours,
With each gentle pull, dreams entwine,
In the rhythm of the ocean's line.

Beneath the surface, a world awakes,
From starlit depths, the heartbeat quakes,
Every ripple, a promise made,
In the dance of shadows, dreams cascade.

While sailors sleep, the waters hum,
Ancient tales of what will come,
The whispers swell beneath the foam,
In the submerged harvest, they find home.

Enchantment in the Coral Grove

In the heart of the deep, where colors bloom,
Lies a grove sealed in soft perfume,
Coral branches stretch to greet the sun,
In this hidden place, the magic's spun.

Mermaids linger in twilight's gleam,
With laughter woven through a dream,
They weave the tales that tides compose,
In glittering gardens where wonder grows.

Shapes of wonders, lost and found,
Spin in spirals as currents surround,
In the embrace of the ocean's sigh,
Echoes of dreams rise, never to die.

Beneath the azure, secrets hide,
In the coral grove where spirits glide,
Each shimmer sings of stories past,
In this enchanted realm, dreams are cast.

So wander here, where the heart can thrive,
In a coral grove where magic's alive,
Let the wonders flow, let the spirit roam,
For in this haven, you'll find your home.

Grain Fields Adrift in Blue

Golden grains on ocean's edge,
Waves caress with gentle pledge,
Fields of amber meet the tide,
In the blue where dreams reside.

The salty breeze brings whispers near,
Of harvests sung with joy and cheer,
Underneath the vast expanse,
Life dances in a timeless trance.

Seagulls wheel through the fragrant air,
In hues of dusk, they seem to care,
For every seed that finds its way,
In the embrace of night and day.

Each swell of blue holds stories spun,
Of golden fields, of battles won,
As water weaves through stalks so high,
Nature's canvas, a quiet sigh.

So gaze upon this golden scene,
Where land and ocean intertwine, serene,
In grain fields adrift, hope does bloom,
In the gentle stretch of nature's room.

Enigmas of Flora Beneath the Sea

In depths of blue, where secrets lie,
Coral gardens bloom beneath the sigh.
Whispers of kelp sway with the tide,
Each creature plays in this ocean ride.

Anemone dances, soft and bright,
Protecting friends in a shimmering light.
Clownfish dart in playful delight,
As shadows mingle with the gentle night.

A seahorse wanders, regal and true,
Among the sea fans, emerald and blue.
Mysteries deepen, the currents weave,
Stories untold beneath the eave.

With every wave, a tale unfolds,
Of ancient realms and treasures bold.
The sea is a book, pages unwritten,
In its embrace, we are all smitten.

Yet whispers warn of care and grace,
For in this beauty, dangers chase.
Respect the depths, where wonders gleam,
In the heart of the ocean, we find our dream.

Salt Harvests and Ocean Dreams

When dawn awakens with a blush,
The fishermen gather, in morning hush.
With nets in hand, they cast their dreams,
In salty waves, the ocean gleams.

Crisp air carries laughter and song,
As seagulls dance where they belong.
Catch of the day, a feast to share,
The tides provide, the heart laid bare.

Shells and treasures washed ashore,
A bounty awaits, forevermore.
With every wave, a secret found,
In salt-laden winds, their hopes abound.

Sunset paints the sky with fire,
Igniting passions that never tire.
Ocean dreams breathe life anew,
A kingdom vast, eternally true.

As stars emerge in velvet sky,
Fishermen's wishes take to the high.
In the echoes of waves, they find their realm,
In salt harvests, the sea at the helm.

The Sorgen of Wavy Meadows

In fields that sway like whispering seas,
Where flowers dance in the summer breeze.
Golden grains ripple, shadows play,
Nature's canvas, where dreams sway.

Underneath the arch of cerulean skies,
The sun dips low, a sweet surprise.
Fields of worry, of hopes and fears,
In every heartbeat, the meadow hears.

Beneath each blade, a tale unfolds,
Of laughter shared and hands that hold.
Soft whispers call from a distant place,
In every corner, a sacred space.

As twilight drapes its velvet veil,
The meadow sighs, a gentle trail.
In the hush of dusk, worries cease,
Embraced by the night, we find our peace.

With morning light, the cycle spins,
Renewed by grace, as each day begins.
The Sorgen linger, but hope will grow,
In wavy meadows, our spirits flow.

Currents Lapping at Golden Fields

Where river meets the land so wide,
Currents roll with graceful pride.
Waves of grain in tandem sway,
Nature's rhythm, night and day.

Secrets carried on the breeze,
Whispers soft among the trees.
Golden fields stretch far and high,
Kissing blue beneath the sky.

Moist earth cradles roots of dreams,
Nourished by sun, enriched by streams.
Each grain a story, each stalk a song,
A tapestry of life, where we belong.

As the sunset spills its pearly light,
Fields aglow, an enchanting sight.
Currents dance, the air so sweet,
In golden realms, our hearts repeat.

In every rustle, a promise shared,
In golden fields, we're gently cared.
With every lap of nature's hand,
We find our place in this vast land.

Under Aqua Canopies of Amber Harvest

Beneath the surface, realms unfold,
Where whispers dance, the tales are told.
Golden leaves, like oceans wide,
In currents soft, our secrets bide.

Amber fingers, reaching down,
Caress the depths, a gentle crown.
In waters deep, where memories gleam,
Harvest dreams, like silver stream.

Echoes whisper, shadows sway,
In every tide, a heart's ballet.
Amongst the boughs of sea and sky,
Under canopies, we drift and fly.

Translucent bonds, where spirits meet,
In coral gardens, love's heartbeat.
With gentle grace, the waves return,
For every tale, a spark to burn.

In twilight's glow, we stand aligned,
With nature's secrets, intertwined.
Under aqua canopies, the world is spun,
In amber harvest, our journey's begun.

Beneath the Waves

Beneath the waves, the whispers play,
In dreams of blue, we drift away.
Secrets swim from shore to shore,
In silent depths, we seek for more.

With every ripple, ancient calls,
In hidden caves where twilight falls.
The dance of light, a fleeting trace,
In ocean's arms, we find our place.

Life beneath, a mystic weave,
In currents bold, we dare believe.
From sandy beds to rocky crests,
In every tide, our spirit rests.

With coral reefs, a vibrant hue,
They tell the tales of me and you.
In watery realms, a love will bloom,
As starfish twirl within the gloom.

In every wave that crashes loud,
A promise made to join the crowd.
Beneath the waves, our spirits soar,
Together forever, forevermore.

Secrets of the Fields

In golden fields where shadows hide,
The whispers flow like a gentle tide.
Secrets linger in the rustling grass,
Beneath the sky, our moments pass.

Time stands still in sunlit dreams,
Where laughter twirls in golden beams.
Each leaf a story, every bloom,
In fragrant air, we chase our gloom.

Footprints mark the paths we tread,
With every step, our hearts have bled.
But in the quiet, hope takes flight,
In fields of gold, we find the light.

The humble soil, a friend so dear,
In every season, it will reappear.
Beneath the sun, the shadows blend,
In whispered fields, we make our mend.

With grains of solace, life will rise,
In fallen leaves, a sweet surprise.
Secrets of the fields, forever known,
In earth's embrace, we have grown.

Nurtured by Moonlit Tides

Nurtured by moonlit tides so bright,
We dance along the edge of night.
In silver beams, our dreams take flight,
As waves caress the shores of light.

The ocean sings a lullaby,
Beneath a canvas, vast and shy.
In salty winds, our hopes will soar,
With every wave, we long for more.

The horizon glows with secrets deep,
As starlit waters cradle sleep.
With tidal rhythms, hearts align,
In the embrace of the divine.

Each surge of tide, a lover's call,
In moonlit whispers, we give our all.
As constellations weave their song,
Nurtured here, we both belong.

From beach to bay, our spirits gleam,
In every shadow, love's bright dream.
Nurtured by the tides so free,
In moonlit dance, it's you and me.

Salted Secrets of the Mystic Garden

In gardens lush, where secrets dwell,
Salted winds weave their magic spell.
Petals whisper to the morning dew,
In vibrant hues, they call to you.

Mystic paths where shadows glide,
In every corner, joys abide.
With hidden nooks of sweet delight,
Beneath the canopy of night.

Every blossom holds a tale,
Of wanderers lost, of lovers pale.
In fragrant air, the past awakes,
As laughter dances, the silence breaks.

Salted secrets on the breeze,
In every rustle, nature frees.
With gentle hands, the earth we sow,
In mystic gardens, together we grow.

From roots below to skies above,
In every petal, a sign of love.
Salted secrets gently lay,
In this paradise, we find our way.

Maritime Silhouettes and Grainy Shadows

In twilight's embrace, the ships slowly drift,
Beneath the horizon, where secrets uplift.
Glimmers of starlight weave through the night,
Casting silhouettes in the soft, fading light.

The waves whisper tales of the deep, unknown,
Of sailors and mermaids, in dreams they have sown.
Grainy shadows dance on the ocean's expanse,
With each gentle swell, they invite a glance.

Secrets of ages flow with the tide,
In crevices hidden, where forgotten things bide.
Maritime whispers, a symphony low,
Echoing softly wherever we go.

Idealistic visions where sea meets the shore,
In the hush of the dusk, I find I want more.
For all that has been, and all that will be,
The ocean's embrace holds the heart of the sea.

Algae Blossoms in Golden Currents

In the twilight glimmer, green swirls arise,
Algae blossoms beneath softening skies.
They sway with the currents, dancing with grace,
Painting the waters in an emerald lace.

Golden currents flow where secrets may hide,
With stories of oceans where wonders reside.
Each twist of the wave, a whisper, a song,
As the heart of the sea plays all summer long.

Journeys unfold in this liquid embrace,
Where creatures of magic drift through empty space.
Algae and laughter merge in the spray,
As tides carry dreams of adventure away.

Infinite patterns create a grand show,
In undulating rhythms, where breezes may blow.
Here in this realm, we are lost and found,
With nature's soft sighs, in harmony drown.

Luminescent Flora of the Abyss

In the depths of darkness, a glow softly beams,
Luminescent flora weave fantastical dreams.
With colors that pulse in the silence of deep,
They guard all the secrets the ocean must keep.

Dancing like fireflies in the midnight's embrace,
They light up the shadows, bring life to this space.
Beneath the cold waves where sunlight won't tread,
These flowers of magic paint life where we dread.

Coral companions in shimmering hues,
Dance to the tune of the ghosts of the blues.
A ballet of beauty in silence they thrive,
In the heart of the abyss, they keep hope alive.

When wonders and whispers collide in the night,
The ocean unveils its ephemeral light.
Each bloom is a story, each flicker a tale,
In the depths of the sea, where living prevails.

Melodies from the Underwater Orchard

Beneath the blue waves, a symphony plays,
With melodies hidden in the ocean's embrace.
Each note like a ripple, each chord a delight,
From the underwater orchard, a magical sight.

Fish glide like dancers, in tuneful delight,
While seaweed sways gently, embracing the night.
The rhythm of currents creates a sweet song,
As creatures of wonder join in the throng.

In caverns of coral, the harmonies swell,
Where the sounds of the sea craft a fluid spell.
Echoes of laughter mix soft with the tide,
In an orchestra played where the mysteries glide.

With shells as their instruments, they play with finesse,
A timeless performance, nature's own mess.
And as waves gently break, their chorus will soar,
Carrying tales of the ocean's great lore.

The Lure of Aquatic Amber Echoes

In the depths where shadows dwell,
Amber echoes softly swell,
Whispers of the ocean's heart,
Calling forth each hidden part.

Ghostly ships and treasures lost,
In the waves they count the cost,
Seashells sing of tales untold,
Of ancient legends, brave and bold.

Beneath the waves, secrets lie,
Glimmers of a sunlit sky,
Mysterious currents ebb and flow,
An allure that weaves its glow.

The laughter of the fish resounds,
In liquid realms and echoing sounds,
Close your eyes and dive within,
To find the magic, let it begin.

Aquatic dreams enchant the night,
Where amber glimmers meet the light,
Adventures wait in depths serene,
In this world of twinkling green.

Whispers of Grain in Ocean Depths

In the quiet of the brine,
Grains of gold like sunbeam shine,
They dance upon the ocean floor,
Whispers beckon, urging more.

Waves of harvest touch the shore,
Merging sea and land, explore,
Tales of fields and salty spray,
Grains of life in wild ballet.

Seagulls call, the breezes tell,
Of ancient lands where grains fell,
Where bread and bounty meet the sea,
Feeding hearts with harmony.

In the depths where waters weave,
Nature's tapestry, believe,
Harvest moonlight starts to glow,
In each grain, a tale to sow.

Ocean's breath, a sweet embrace,
In every wave, a sacred space,
Whispers of grain, forever blend,
An endless cycle, without end.

Sands of Time with Sea's Abundance

Waves caress the shores of dreams,
Sands of time and silver gleams,
Tides that rhythmically unfold,
Stories lost and tales retold.

Drifting grains that slip away,
Mark the sunset of each day,
Footsteps fade upon the shore,
Yet the ocean keeps its score.

Shells and treasures washed in light,
Carried forth from depths of night,
In the bounty of the tide,
Time itself begins to glide.

With each wave that gently breaks,
The sea whispers what it makes,
Crafted from the dusk and dawn,
A cornucopia, reborn.

So let the sands of time unfold,
As stories of the sea are told,
In its cradle, life abounds,
In every rhythm, spirit grounds.

Cornucopia of Coral and Crop

Coral gardens softly sway,
In the ocean's bright ballet,
With colors bold and life anew,
A feast of blessings, ever true.

Underneath the waves' embrace,
Fields of coral find their place,
Harvest moons above them shine,
Nature's bounty, so divine.

Fishermen and farmers meet,
In a union, strong and sweet,
Sharing wealth from land and sea,
In this bond, we're truly free.

Crops that flourish, waters thrive,
In this cornucopia, we dive,
Together, hand in hand we stand,
United by both sea and land.

So let us dance with joy and cheer,
For the bounty that draws near,
In every wave, the hopes we sow,
With the coral's brilliant glow.

Fate's Grainy Tokens in Ebbing Tides

In sands where whispers call,
The grains of time do fall,
Each moment etched in light,
A dance of day and night.

Seagulls cry above the bay,
As shadows slip away,
Beneath the silver sky,
We cast our dreams to fly.

Tides wash over tales untold,
In currents fierce and bold,
They carry hopes afar,
To where the wishes are.

With every ebb, a secret fades,
In twilight's soft cascades,
Yet fortune finds its way,
In the stillness of the day.

So gather tokens by the shore,
Let fate restore once more,
For in each grain, a spark,
To light the endless dark.

Reflections on the Edge of the Deep

In waters dark and wide,
The secrets there abide,
Reflections dance and weave,
Inviting hearts to grieve.

Moonlit ripples glide and sway,
As dreams begin to play,
A lullaby to calm the soul,
And make the broken whole.

The sirens sing through whispered night,
In shadows, soft and light,
They beckon with their song,
For a heart that feels so wrong.

And as the waves embrace the shore,
We yearn for something more,
A glimpse of what might be,
A truth that sets us free.

At the edge where hopes reside,
We'll brave the rolling tide,
For even in our fears,
Lie the echoes of our years.

Harvest Moon over Sea and Soil

Beneath the harvest moon's bright glow,
The fields of golden grain do grow,
A tapestry stitched with shadows tall,
Where earth and sea unite, enthrall.

The lapping waves in gentle breath,
Whisper tales of life and death,
As sailors' songs drift through the night,
Each note a spark, a flickered light.

In amber hues, the dusk unfolds,
With secrets held, the world beholds,
The bounty rich, a silent vow,
To share its grace, to humbly bow.

And in the fields, the children play,
While shadows shift at end of day,
With laughter bubbling in the air,
A chorus light, a tapestry rare.

So let us dance beneath this moon,
And sing our hearts in joyful tune,
For nature's gift, forever free,
Is love shared 'twixt the land and sea.

Dancing Ferns in the Ocean Edge

Where ferns do sway with ocean breeze,
And whispers float among the trees,
A magic blooms beneath the sun,
As time and tide weave tales begun.

The salty air, a soft embrace,
Entwining love in this wild place,
With each new wave, a rhythm found,
In nature's beat, our hearts unbound.

The ocean sings a siren's song,
While ferns stand tall and proud, so strong,
They dance upon the shifting sand,
As dreams erupt from this fair land.

So let us twirl with every wave,
While echoes of the sea misbehave,
For in this moment, life takes flight,
And shadows dance in the fading light.

With laughter bright and voices clear,
We flourish here without a fear,
For ferns and waves know deep within,
That joy is where our lives begin.

Burgeoning Flora in Tide's Grip

In the hush where waters sing,
Lilies dance and mermaids cling.
Shells and stones in soft embrace,
Nature weaves her secret lace.

Golden tendrils stretch and sway,
Cradled in the ocean's play.
Beneath the waves, a world awakes,
Life unfolds while silence breaks.

Emerald ferns and corals bright,
Flourish in the fading light.
Whispers of the ebb and flow,
Tell of dreams that come and go.

Among the rocks, a symphony,
Echoes of the deep-set sea.
Colors bleed and rhythms twine,
Crafted by the hand divine.

In this realm of vast surprise,
Magic stirs beneath the skies.
Flora burgeoning, tides that grip,
Life's embrace, a wondrous trip.

Underwater Cradle of Grain and Shell

In the depths where secrets lie,
Grains of sand through fingers fly.
Shells that whisper tales of old,
Cradled in the ocean's fold.

Dappled light through currents glides,
Life awakens where hope bides.
Anemones in vibrant hues,
Beneath the waves, a world imbues.

Seagrass sways, a gentle dance,
In this watery expanse,
Fish and fowl in playful chase,
Open arms of the sea's embrace.

Harvest dreams from tides that ebb,
Where every crevice weaves a web.
Under the surface, magic thrives,
In this cradle, all life strives.

Resting softly, the ocean's chest,
Holds the grains in quiet rest.
Where the world of the waters dwell,
Against the shore, the stories swell.

Elysian Fields Beneath the Blue

In the depths of azure seas,
Elysian fields greet gentle breeze.
Coral reefs like jeweled crowns,
Guard the realms where silence drowns.

Bubbles rise from creatures small,
In harmony, they heed the call.
Starfish glide on oceans' flow,
Among the wonders hidden low.

Whales sing in melodic tune,
A lullaby by the silver moon.
In this realm of untold grace,
Life flourishes in wondrous space.

Crabs scuttle with a hurried charm,
Seeking safety from all harm.
Anemones sway with vibrant flair,
Creating fields beyond compare.

As tides embrace the shimming shore,
Elysium awaits forevermore.
Where the blue and golden blend,
Life begins and never ends.

Nuances of the Tidal Grain

Waves caress the sable sand,
In motion like a painter's hand.
Grains of tide-touched quiet fate,
Whisper tales of love and fate.

Textures shift as seasons wane,
Kisses from the sea's domain.
In this dance, time's whisper flows,
Life unfurls as the curtain grows.

Starry shells underfoot lie,
Echoing the ocean's sigh.
Every grain a story spun,
Tales of shadows kissed by sun.

Lapping shores, a rhythmic song,
Where both heart and waves belong.
Nuances of the grains evolve,
In mysteries they dissolve.

With every tide, a breath anew,
In patterns forged beneath the blue.
The world transforms as waters gain,
Life retained in the tidal grain.

Coral Gardens of Earthly Grain

In coral gardens, colors dance,
Where whispers weave in gentle chance.
The ocean's hand, it sows with care,
A tapestry beyond compare.

With currents soft, the secrets gleam,
As sunlight spills a golden beam.
In this realm, the dreams take flight,
Each grain of sand, a starry night.

Here mermaids sing of tales untold,
Of buried treasures, bright and bold.
The sea unfolds her arms wide,
A stunning world where wonders hide.

Among the reefs, the echoes sway,
In harmony, they softly play.
The patience of the tides confides,
The beauty waits where magic bides.

So come, dear soul, to where we tread,
In coral gardens, dreams are spread.
Embrace the warmth, let worries wane,
In earthly grain, true joy we gain.

Sunkissed Shelters Under Water

Beneath the waves, where shadows glide,
Sunkissed shelters, secrets hide.
The gentle sway of kelp and foam,
In watery realms, we find a home.

The shimmering schools, they dart and weave,
In intricate patterns, we believe.
With every ripple, stories bloom,
In sunlit depths, we cast away gloom.

Here memories of laughter dwell,
In echoes soft, we weave our spell.
Under the surface, life abounds,
In harmony, our heart resounds.

Lost in a world of azure hues,
With every stroke, our spirit renews.
Among the corals, love ignites,
In these sunkissed shelters, pure delights.

Come wander with me, let's take the plunge,
In waters deep, we feel the lunge.
With open hearts, we'll slip away,
To where the sunbeams dance and play.

Tales from the Grainy Abyss

In the grainy abyss where shadows dwell,
Ancient whispers weave a spell.
Cradle your fears, let them take flight,
In the depths where stars ignite.

The siren's call, it softly sings,
Of forgotten dreams and fragile things.
With pearl-like tears, the ocean weeps,
For secrets lost in endless deeps.

Through murky waters, legends rise,
In shimmering depths, the heart complies.
Each tale is spun with salt and sand,
A fleeting touch of time's own hand.

From grainy shadows, hopes emerge,
In whispered tones, the tides converge.
We sail on currents of the past,
In this timeless sea, our fates are cast.

So listen close, dear sailor brave,
In the abyss, the lost will save.
With every wave, a story's told,
In the grainy depths, we find our gold.

Siren's Harvest of Sunlit Grain

In fields of gold where sirens sing,
A harvest waits for echoing spring.
With every voice that fills the air,
The promise blooms without a care.

The talons clutch at grains of light,
As day meets dusk in soft twilight.
Glistening paths, the songbirds trace,
In unity, we find our place.

The ripples dance, the sunbeams flow,
In this embrace, our spirits grow.
With laughter shared beneath the sun,
Together, we become as one.

Through golden fields, we weave a dream,
A tapestry of all that gleams.
With hearts aglow, we shall remain,
In siren's harvest of sunlit grain.

So let us wander, hand in hand,
Through golden seas of shimmering sand.
In every whisper, nature's song,
In love's embrace, we all belong.

Harvests of the Deep

In twilight's glow, the waves do sigh,
With whispers of treasures that float and fly.
Beneath the crests, where silence dwells,
The ocean's heart, a tale retells.

Seashells gather like secrets old,
Each grain of sand, a story told.
With nets cast wide, the fishermen dream,
Of shimmering bounties and silver's gleam.

The tides dance forth with rhythmic grace,
As moonlight kisses the water's face.
From depths unknown, the heroes rise,
Braving the currents, chasing the skies.

In every wave, a promise lies,
A spark of wonder beneath blue skies.
The ocean's lore, both fierce and sweet,
Carries the echoes of time's heartbeat.

So venture forth, oh brave and kind,
For treasures await where dreams unwind.
In harvests deep, our souls shall sing,
Of all the magic the oceans bring.

Secrets Beneath the Surface

In the tranquil depths, shadows play,
With secrets woven in shades of gray.
The silence hums a haunting tune,
Beneath the watchful eye of the moon.

Coral cradles the dreams of old,
In pasta shells and treasures bold.
Each flicker of light, a tale to share,
Of sea-swept journeys floating in air.

Emerald kelp sways to the beat,
Guarding whispers in a dark retreat.
What lies beyond, we yearn to know,
In the hidden realms where echoes flow.

With shimmering scales that glint and gleam,
Mirrors of magic in a sailor's dream.
The deep is alive with laughter and screams,
A tapestry stitched with rippling dreams.

To seek the truths that dwell below,
In currents strong and undertows.
From darkness once feared, let wonder arise,
For secrets are gifts in the ocean's guise.

Echoes of Ocean's Bounty

Upon the shore, the gulls do cry,
As waves weave tales where waters lie.
Each tide that rolls, a song so sweet,
Echoes of bounty beneath our feet.

Seaweed dancers in hues of green,
Move with grace in a watery scene.
The sunbeams kiss the ocean's face,
A moment of stillness, pure embrace.

Driftwood whispers of travels long,
In each splintered edge, a sailor's song.
The anchor's weight, a memory's claim,
In salt and spray, we find our name.

Mysterious caves that beckon the brave,
Hold stories of life, of loss, and save.
With every treasure from depths below,
The ocean gifts us what we must know.

So gather the echoes, dear heart, don't flee,
For in each return, there's magic to see.
The bounty of life, a vast, open sea,
Whispers of dreams where we long to be.

Tides of Grain and Myth

Where ocean meets land, the legends flow,
In tides that carry both truth and woe.
The grains of gold upon the shore,
Keep company with tales of yore.

Breezes whisper of knights and kings,
In the rustle of reeds, their triumphs sing.
For every shell, a journey starts,
Woven with hope in sunlit arts.

The moon's soft pull draws ships to dream,
With silver sails and starlit beam.
Each wave that crashes brings forth the past,
The tides of myth, forever vast.

Oh, mysteries wrapped in the salty air,
In stories shared, our hearts ensnare.
From grains of sand to horizons wide,
We find our path on the swelling tide.

So heed the call of the ocean's breath,
For in its depths lies life and death.
A dance of fate, both bold and sly,
In the heart of the sea, our spirits fly.

Twilight Whispers of Aquatic Harvest

In twilight's glow, the waters gleam,
Where silvery fish dart, a fleeting dream.
Ripples dance in the evening tide,
While the moon whispers secrets that cannot hide.

Soft shadows gather, sweet with the scent,
Of salty breezes, the sea's lament.
Barnacles cling to the ancient stone,
A tale of the ocean, forever sown.

Lighthouses gleam through misty embrace,
Guiding the vessels, they travel apace.
With each crashing wave, a story unfolds,
Of sailors brave and treasures of old.

Nautical dreams rise like the sun,
In waters deep, the harvest begun.
With every tide, we listen and learn,
From whispers of twilight, our passions burn.

Shimmering Sands and Amber Brews

Under the sun, the sands do shine,
Golden grains, so pure, divine.
Waves caress the shore with grace,
While memories linger in time and space.

Amber brews in shaded nooks,
Spirits rise from weathered books.
Secrets of old in every sip,
As stories twist in gentle trip.

Dunes shift softly in the warm embrace,
Of whispers carried in a sunbeam's race.
The ocean hums a melodic tune,
As twilight descends, invoking the moon.

Each star ignites an ancient lore,
A journey across the ocean's floor.
Where dreams of adventure begin anew,
In shimmering sands, and brews of brew.

Breath of the Tides and Riches Untold

The breath of the tides, a lullaby sung,
Carries the tales of the young and the sprung.
From depths unknown, where sea creatures roam,
Riches untold find their way home.

Seashells whisper of journeys afar,
Guiding the dreamers beneath the stars.
Each cresting wave a fortune does bear,
With treasures hidden in oceanic care.

As gulls cry out, a serenade free,
The winds weave stories of all that can be.
In the dance of the sea, life flows and spools,
A symphony played by the watery jewels.

As horizons blend in twilight's caress,
A treasure trove of boundless success.
With each breath of the tides, hope does unfold,
Stories of beauty and riches untold.

Merfolk's Embrace of the Golden Fields

In golden fields where shadows play,
Merfolk gather at the end of day.
With laughter ringing, they weave their song,
A tapestry bright, where they all belong.

Beneath the waves, their spirits glide,
In harmony with the ebbing tide.
They share their tales with land and sea,
In hopes of a world where all can be free.

Fields of daisies sway in the breeze,
A witness to laughter beneath the trees.
With every secret the twilight furthers,
They find a bond that gently hovers.

In the embrace of the moonlit night,
Merfolk dance, a mesmerizing sight.
Their joy ripples through land and sky,
A bridge between worlds where dreams cannot die.

So let us gather, hand in hand,
In the magic of moments we understand.
For in every heart, there lies a thread,
Of merfolk's embrace, where dreams are bred.

Ears of Gold Beneath the Waves

Ears of gold sway in the foam,
Whispers dance where sea creatures roam.
Beneath the surface, secrets dwell,
In shimmering shells, they weave their spell.

Tides of silver, kissed by the sun,
Murmurs of magic, a tale begun.
Echoes of laughter, the ocean sings,
Carving stories in the hearts of kings.

The seaweed brushes, soft and light,
Calling the dreamers, ghosts of the night.
With each gentle wave, a promise unfolds,
Of treasures forever, and legends untold.

Winds carry tales from the far, deep sea,
In the realm of the lost, we long to be free.
Ears of gold glow in the moon's pale gleam,
Entwined in the currents of a sailor's dream.

So cast your nets into the blue mist,
For within the current, your fate may be kissed.
In the deep embrace of the ocean's fold,
You may find the wonders of ears of gold.

Silken Shores of Harvest Dreams

On silken shores where the shadows play,
Dreams of harvests waltz and sway.
A gentle breeze brings scents so sweet,
As tides of gold embrace our feet.

Fields of wheat beneath the twilight glow,
Whispers of magic in the undertow.
Beneath the starlight, hopes unfurl,
In silken sands, treasures swirl.

Joyful laughter rides the winds' warm breath,
In the heart of summer, life conquers death.
Where grains of wisdom meet the sea,
In the arms of the earth, we dream to be free.

Gathering whispers like seeds to sow,
In the garden of time, let memories grow.
Silken shores call with a siren's tune,
In moonlit nights, we'll cherish their boon.

So dance with the tides as they take their flight,
In the golden harvest's shimmering light.
For on these shores where our dreams recline,
We'll find the magic, forever divine.

The Siren's Grainy Whisper

In shadows of dusk, where the wild waves rise,
The siren's call weaves a tangled guise.
Her grainy whisper, so soft, yet clear,
Pulls at the heart, drawing wanderers near.

With hair of seafoam and eyes of the sky,
She sings of journeys, of love gone awry.
Songs of the ocean bring warmth and despair,
Casting a spell on the hearts that dare.

Through currents and eddies, her stories flow,
In the salt of the sea, our dreams come and go.
Grains of remembrance drift on the tides,
In the depths of our souls, where magic abides.

So heed the call of the sea's sweet song,
For within her embrace, we've all belonged.
The grainy whispers, like grains of sand,
They sculpt our fates, they blend with our hands.

As the stars emerge from the night's warm veil,
The siren's laughter rides each silver trail.
Her whispers linger, both haunting and bright,
In the heart of the sea, we find our light.

Aqua Harvests in Dusk's Embrace

In dusk's embrace, where shadows dance,
Aqua harvests sway in a silvery trance.
Rippling waters hold secrets untold,
As night descends, revealing pure gold.

Beneath the surface, life weaves and twirls,
In the depths of the ocean, a mosaic unfurls.
Fishermen's nets gleam with stories of yore,
Catching moments that fate can restore.

Moonlight glimmers on each curling wave,
Hints of adventure, the bold and the brave.
Aqua colors bleeding with dreams to embrace,
In the spectral light, we find our place.

So gather your courage, set sail with the tide,
For within the dusk, the magic won't hide.
Harvest the moments, as they gently fall,
In aqua depths, hear the ocean's call.

As the stars beckon, dance on the sea,
In dusk's warm embrace, we yearn to be free.
Together we'll weave with the silk of the night,
In aqua harvests, we'll bask in the light.

Echoes of the Aquatic Grove

In shadows deep where soft dreams dwell,
Whispers of currents weave a spell.
Leaves dance lightly in the blue,
While secrets murmur, old yet new.

Beneath the crest of shimmering light,
Creatures stir in the velvet night.
Pebbles nudge, and tendrils sway,
Calling forth the dawn of day.

Eldritch notes rise from ocean's heart,
Nature's magic, a timeless art.
Here love blossoms in every seam,
Under the veil of a sailor's dream.

The waters hum a lullaby,
As wonders drift and spirits fly.
Each echo carries stories past,
Through realms of peace that forever last.

So linger near where silence sings,
And feel the joy that living brings.
In the grove where the waters sigh,
Your heart will learn to swim and fly.

Glistening Fields Beneath the Waves

Beneath the froth and dancing spray,
Fields of glittering dreams at play.
Emerald fronds kiss the tide,
In a world where wonders abide.

Softly twinkling, secrets long,
In seaweed's grasp, a siren's song.
Here light cascades in silver beams,
And shadows waltz with fragile dreams.

Creatures flit like glimpses rare,
Through gardens dressed in liquid air.
Fish flicker like comet trails,
As nostalgia swims, and time exhales.

Coral crowns that touch the deep,
Guarding the treasures we must keep.
In every wave, a tale unfolds,
Of joy and heartache, bright and bold.

So dive, dear heart, into the tides,
Where glistening fields of magic reside.
Beneath the waves, let spirits soar,
In the echoes of forevermore.

Golden Secrets in Maritime Depths

In depths where sunlight scarcely probes,
Golden secrets weave their robes.
Ancient maps whisper of lore,
Echoes of ships that sailed before.

Glistening grains of sand do hold,
Stories spun in threads of gold.
From the heart of the ocean wide,
Mysteries swell on the turning tide.

Treasures lie in forgotten hulls,
Cradled soft in ocean's lulls.
Beside the wrecks, lost dreams still gleam,
In this liquid realm of forgotten dreams.

Sirens sing to draw hearts near,
With notes that tangle in the ear.
Tales of love and longing lost,
In the whirlpool's embrace, we pay the cost.

So search the depths with curious eye,
For golden truths that shimmer nigh.
In maritime realms of deep regret,
Life's vibrant pulse we shall not forget.

Celestial Sown Sands of the Ocean Floor

Upon the sands where stars descend,
Celestial seeds of dreams extend.
Each grain a wish, a hope, a prayer,
Scattered wide in the ocean's care.

Softly shifting, the tides do weave,
Tales of those who dare believe.
In the silent realms of sapphire blue,
Lies the promise of all we pursue.

Coral gardens burst with light,
As constellations dance in sight.
Down below, the cosmos twirls,
Within the depths, enchantment swirls.

Waves lap gently at hidden dreams,
Carrying whispers on silver beams.
Each heartbeat echoes through the swell,
Of stories only the ocean can tell.

So wander far on sown sands bright,
And seek the magic beyond the light.
In celestial splendor let hope explore,
The depths where dreams forever soar.

The Nautical Harvest Dance

Beneath the crescent moon's soft glow,
The waves sway gently to and fro.
With lanterns lit, the barn doors wide,
The sailors' tunes on the night tide.

With laughter rich like summer's sun,
They spin and twirl, each heart a drum.
From bow to stern, their joy spills free,
In rhythm with the endless sea.

Whispers of salt in the evening breeze,
Dancing shadows beneath the trees.
With every step, the ocean sings,
Beneath the stars, a dream takes wing.

Folk and fish in a merry chase,
Joined by tides, they find their place.
As Neptune smiles from his watery throne,
Together they harvest what's sea-folk grown.

As dawn breaks o'er the silver foam,
They gather treasures, then head for home.
With spirits high, the night must cease,
In waves of joy, they find their peace.

Mermaid's Treasure in Fields of Sun

In golden fields where daisies dance,
A mermaid whispers of an old romance.
Fresh blooms of lavender fill the air,
Her voice like honey, sweet and rare.

Beneath the sun, the treasures shine,
Shells from depths where the currents twine.
Each grain of sand, a story spun,
Of moonlit nights and a day well done.

The waves bring secrets, old and wise,
While fireflies weave their sparkling ties.
Mermaid's laughter, light and free,
In harmony with the land and sea.

From ocean's depth to verdant plain,
Her treasure trove, a sweet refrain.
With every whisper, the world awakes,
A story told as daylight breaks.

The sun bows low, the evening sighs,
Her dance continues where the horizon lies.
In fields of sun, the magic grows,
As mermaids weave through twilight's glow.

Saltwater Threads in Amber Corn

In fields where amber grains wave high,
Saltwater threads weave a lullaby.
The ocean's breath, a gentle sigh,
Calls to the harvest as gulls fly by.

Fingers of sun trace the golden stalks,
While whispers of sea weave through the walks.
Every ear of corn holds a tale,
Of tempest storms and wind's soft wail.

Through ripening husks, the secrets hum,
Of tides that crash, of hearts that drum.
In ceaseless dance, they yield their grace,
As squall and sunbillow embrace.

The farmer's hands, so skilled and true,
Gather the salt, the earth, the blue.
With each new dawn, the harvest gleams,
A tapestry stitched with sea-born dreams.

At dusk, the colors burst and blend,
With salty kisses the oceans send.
In amber light, the treasures gleam,
As nature spins its wondrous dream.

Currents of Grain on a Silver Shore

Where waves embrace the silver shore,
Currents of grain hum evermore.
Underneath the skies of blue,
Whispers of the wind speak true.

Frosty morns with amber tide,
Fields and oceans sing with pride.
Harvesters tread on swaying land,
Waving to the sea, a gentle hand.

Nature's bounty, wild and pure,
Where grains of gold endure.
Oceans blend with fields of green,
In every corner, magic's seen.

Currents wrap the earth in song,
Binding hearts to where they belong.
As twilight dances on each crest,
The grain and sea find their rest.

Reflections cast in evening's light,
Upon the shore, both dark and bright.
In harmony, their spirits soar,
In currents of grain on the silver shore.

Echoes of Green in the Tidal Currents

In whispers soft, the tides play low,
With echoes of green that ebb and flow.
Driftwood dances in the salt-kissed air,
And secrets hum, alive with care.

Beneath the waves, a treasure lies,
Where sunlight flickers, and silence sighs.
Anemones sway in rhythm divine,
Time's gentle current, an endless line.

Fishermen's dreams on vessels pale,
Set sail for shores where stories sail.
Each catch a tale, each rippling grace,
Celebrating life in this watery place.

Mossy banks cradle seeds as they sleep,
In nature's bower, promises deep.
Footprints linger on the sandy shore,
While laughter echoes forevermore.

With every tide, a cycle begins,
The dance of nature, where love never ends.
In the heart of the sea, green whispers blend,
Echoes of magic as waters descend.

Seagrass and Fields Unite

Where sea meets the meadow, a symphony grows,
Seagrass and fields which the soft wind blows.
Rustling whispers in the evening light,
Earth and ocean in a warm embrace tight.

Coral blooms paint a canvas of dreams,
While golden grains shimmer with sunlight beams.
A ballet of textures, both soft and rough,
In every touch, they blend yet stay tough.

Crabs scuttle over the sand in retreat,
As daisies nod where the blue waves meet.
Water and earth in a sweet duet,
Binding their spirits in endless net.

Murmurs of shells, stories within,
Tales of the deep where wonders begin.
As starlight spills on the oceans wide,
Seagrass and fields, forever abide.

The horizon paints whispers of twilight's grace,
Echoes of nature find their place.
In the union of worlds, life finds a way,
As seagrass and fields bring night to the day.

Waves of Grain in Aquatic Realms

On the edge of the earth where the waters swirl,
Waves of grain murmur and gently unfurl.
At dawn's first blush, golden grains awake,
Stretching towards dreams that the sunlight will make.

Like oceans of corn, they sway to the tune,
While crickets chirp under the watch of the moon.
Together they dance to a rhythm unseen,
In harmony woven through landscape serene.

A gust whispers secrets of seasons gone by,
And ripples of time flicker in the sky.
With each passing moment, they breath, they grow,
Waves of golden whispers, their stories flow.

The brook murmurs soft, as it weaves through the fields,
Sprouting bright life while the quivering yields.
Glorious and grand in this vibrant array,
Both waves and grains join in nature's ballet.

And as the sun dips, casting hues of fire,
The night strolls in, beneath its desire.
Offering peace to the land and the sea,
In waves of grain, the world finds its key.

Ocean's Bounty at Twilight's Door

In the hush of twilight, the ocean sighs,
Painting the sky with its soft goodbyes.
Bounty abounds where the shadows creep,
Secrets held tight in the ocean's deep.

Driftwood tells tales of journeys afar,
While shimmering fish become the evening stars.
The ebb and flow in a tender embrace,
Whispers of magic in this sacred place.

As the sun sinks low, a gem of a glow,
Seafoam and stardust in a soft undertow.
The world takes a breath as day meets the night,
In ocean's bounty, everything feels right.

Shells hold the echoes of waves long past,
Each grain of sand a story cast.
Nature's artistry blooms in the dim,
Stars awaken, and lullabies brim.

At twilight's door, where the sea meets land,
Moments like pearls slip through our hands.
With every heartbeat, a story we share,
In the ocean's bounty, we find our care.

Driftwood and Barley Dreams

Whispers of the sea, they call,
Driftwood floats, a gentle thrall.
Barley fields sway soft and low,
In twilight's glow, their secrets flow.

Ghostly tides, they lap and learn,
Carrying tales of flame and fern.
Through briny breeze, sweet dreams do sweep,
Where time and tide in silence creep.

Stars alight on golden waves,
With stories of the lost and brave.
In the amber light they shine,
A world where fate and hope entwine.

Footprints carved in shifting sand,
Echoes of an unseen hand.
The driftwood bears both joy and pain,
In barley dreams, all hope remains.

Beneath the moon, the shadows dance,
A woven tale, a fleeting glance.
With each soft tide, new dreams are spun,
As hearts awaken, one by one.

Remnants of Oceanic Abundance

In twilight's grasp, the ocean sighs,
Collecting whispers, deep and wise.
With every wave, a treasure found,
The remnants speak, both sweet and sound.

Seashells scatter like silken dreams,
Reflecting sunlight's golden beams.
Tides carry tales from far-off lands,
A symphony played by unseen hands.

From briny depths, lost hopes arise,
In shimmering mists, beneath the skies.
Each droplet holds a story old,
Of journeys gone, and fables told.

Currents dance with a playful grace,
As seabirds flit, in sky's embrace.
The foam doth weave a silken thread,
Binding the dreams of those long dead.

In this vast world, we play our part,
As waves of life encircle the heart.
For in the ocean's deep expanse,
Lie remnants of long-lost romance.

Dance of the Grain-Eyed Sirens

In fields of gold, the sirens sing,
With voices soft, like winds in spring.
Each grain a glimmer, a beckoning light,
Summoning souls who dance through the night.

Their laughter twirls in the autumn air,
Weaving spells without a care.
For grain-eyed visions entice the heart,
As harvest moon begins to impart.

Among the stalks, shadows entwine,
Lost in the echoes of love divine.
With each soft sway, the magic grows,
A tapestry spun where the wild wind blows.

In twilight's hush, their song unfolds,
A glimpse of dreams in shades of gold.
They call to wanderers, lost and brave,
To join the dance on the silken wave.

With whispers sweet, they lead us near,
To realms where laughter drowns all fear.
In grain-eyed worlds, forever roam,
As sirens guide us safely home.

Seafoam and Harvest Moon

Under the moon, the seafoam gleams,
A radiant glow that softly beams.
Harvest whispers on the night breeze,
Tales of joy beneath the trees.

The tides roll in with stories new,
Under the skies of endless blue.
Each wave that crashes on the shore,
Brings echoes of the days before.

In sea and salt, the world doth twine,
Love and loss, in perfect line.
Beneath the moon's watchful eye,
Heroes rise and shadows sigh.

Fields of grain in moonlight dance,
A fleeting glimpse, a lover's glance.
Seafoam mingling with dreams of old,
A tapestry of heartbeats bold.

And as the night folds into dawn,
We gather hopes, reborn, drawn on.
With every tide, a chance to glean,
In seafoam hues, our souls serene.

Glistening Fields of Ocean's Harvest

In fields of waves, the harvest gleams,
Where silver fish dance in sunlit streams.
Tides whisper secrets, stories untold,
A treasure of wonders, shimmering gold.

Seagulls cry out, their shadows glide,
Over sandy shores, where memories hide.
Baskets brim full, with bounty divine,
In the glistening fields, their lives intertwine.

Crabs scuttle by, in a hurried race,
While gentle breezes caress the face.
The ocean breathes out, a melody sweet,
In harmony woven, where land and sea meet.

Sunset paints hues of orange and red,
As fishermen sing, their nets overhead.
The day bids farewell, with a soft sigh,
In glistening fields, where dreams never die.

Echoing Shells and Grainy Tales

Each shell a story whispers so clear,
Of tides that have traveled far and near.
Grains of sand, underfoot they lay,
Carrying secrets of yesterday.

Waves crash and roll, a rhythmic beat,
As children build castles, so grand, so sweet.
Echoes of laughter blend with the tide,
In the heart of the ocean, where treasures abide.

The moon casts shadows on the surface bright,
While dreamers wander through the warm night.
In the glow of the stars, they find their way,
Echoing shells lead where the wishes play.

Stories unfold with the dawn's golden light,
With grainy tales born of the night.
Every whisper and melody swells,
In the dance of the ocean, echoing shells.

The Enchanted Fathoms of Grain

Beneath the waves, the magic thrives,
In enchanted fathoms, where mystery dives.
Grainy treasures linger, softly they weave,
A tapestry spun from the ocean's reprieve.

Coral gardens bloom in colors so rare,
Where fish dart swiftly, they flit, they dare.
A world intertwined, mysterious, bold,
In the depths of the sea, ancient stories unfold.

Shimmering pearls on a bed of soft sighs,
Guarded by currents, beneath the skies.
Each turn a wonder, each swell a song,
In the enchanted fathoms, where echoes belong.

Dancers of seaweed twirl in delight,
Under the watch of the silvery light.
The enchantment breathes in the salt-laden air,
Binding the ocean with magic so rare.

Seaside Secrets of Burgeoning Fields

Amidst the dunes, where wildflowers bloom,
Seaside secrets reveal their soft gloom.
Burgeoning fields stretch, lush and alive,
In the warmth of the sun, the spirits revive.

Waves lap gently, a soothing embrace,
As children explore the vast, open space.
Hidden paths echo with laughter and glee,
In the heart of the seaside's sweet reverie.

Here lie the dreams whispered through leaves,
In the rustling breeze, the heart believes.
Fields of bounty flow under the sky,
Where each moment sings and never will die.

Mornings awaken with hues all aglow,
As the tide dances in, soft and slow.
Nature's canvas, alive and surreal,
Paints the secrets of burgeoning fields.